CHARLES PRENDERGAST  1863–1948

Charles Prendergast in his studio ca. 1918.

# The Art of CHARLES PRENDERGAST

## BY RICHARD J. WATTENMAKER

Distributed by

New York Graphic Society

Greenwich, Connecticut

RUTGERS UNIVERSITY ART GALLERY

MUSEUM OF FINE ARTS, BOSTON

1968

MUSEUM OF FINE ARTS, BOSTON

RUTGERS UNIVERSITY ART GALLERY
New Brunswick, New Jersey

THE PHILLIPS COLLECTION
Washington, D. C.

October 2 – November 3, 1968

November 17 – December 22, 1968

January 11 – February 16, 1969

Cover: Details of cat. no. 52

  Library of Congress Catalogue Card No. 68-9480

Designed by Carl F. Zahn. Printed in West Germany by Brüder Hartmann, Berlin.

Published by Museum of Fine Arts, Boston, and Rutgers, The State University

University Art Gallery Bulletin, Vol. II, No.1

# Acknowledgments

At the outset, we should like to thank all the lenders for allowing their panels to appear in this exhibition. One can only regret, on the artist's behalf, that a number of objects deemed unfit for the rigors of travel were not able to be included. Although many heretofore unknown works are exhibited for the first time and efforts have been made to locate each and every important item, research has failed to uncover a number of panels. It is hoped that one by-product of the present exhibition will be to bring some of these temporarily lost works to light.

For their help in the preparations for the exhibition we should like to thank the following: Leroy Davis; Miss Virginia Fay, Museum of Fine Arts, Boston; John Gordon, Curator, Whitney Museum of American Art; Bartlett H. Hayes, Jr., Director, Addison Gallery of American Art; Mrs. Carole Pesner; Mrs. Duncan Phillips, Director, The Phillips Collection; Charles H. Sawyer, Director, University of Michigan Museum of Art.

A note of thanks is due Mrs. Sadie Zainy for her tireless work on the project.

This publication was, in part, subscribed by the Rutgers University Alumni, Class of 1921. For their outstanding support we should like to express gratitude to Morris M. Ravin, Class Agent, and to John G. Fritzinger, President, Class of 1921.

Special tribute is extended to Antoinette Kraushaar, whose interest in Charles Prendergast through the years has resulted in virtually all of the public recognition accorded the artist over the past thirty-five years. For her generous assistance, without which the present exhibition would not have been possible, we offer our profound thanks.

Most of all, we are fortunate to have had the collaboration and the indispensable assistance of Mrs. Charles Prendergast whose devotion to her husband's art and to his memory has been steadfast through the years.

In the last analysis, whatever is of intrinsic value is, of course, the work of Charles Prendergast.

R. J. W.
P. T. R.

## Lenders to the Exhibition

Mrs. Hamilton Basso
Mr. John Brady, Jr.
Mr. and Mrs. Henry W. Breyer, Jr.
Mr. and Mrs. Granville M. Brumbaugh
Mr. Morris D. Crawford, Jr.
The Rita and Daniel Fraad Collection
Mr. and Mrs. William M. Fuller
Dr. and Mrs. Harold Genvert
Ira and Nancy Glackens
Mr. and Mrs. Frederick L. Good, Jr.
International House, New York
Mr. Elliott Levin
Mrs. Faber Lewis
Mr. and Mrs. Bob London
Mr. and Mrs. John Marin, Jr.
Dr. John J. McDonough
Mr. and Mrs. Philip F. Newman
Mrs. Bliss Parkinson
Mrs. Robert M. Pennoyer
Mrs. Duncan Phillips
Mrs. John W. S. Platt
Mrs. Charles Prendergast
Mrs. J. Woodward Redmond
Mr. and Mrs. Charles H. Sawyer
Estate of Mrs. R. Barclay Scull
Mrs. Thomas Spencer
Tecosky-Schuchar Associates
Mr. John Wilkie
Mrs. Anne Burnett Windfohr
Mr. Robert F. Woolworth
Anonymous

Addison Gallery of American Art,
Phillips Academy, Andover
Museum of Fine Arts, Boston
The Newark Museum
Wadsworth Atheneum, Hartford
Whitney Museum of American Art

# Contents

**1** RISING SUN, 1912

# Foreword

Boston was the birthplace of Charles Prendergast and his home until he and his more famous brother, Maurice, moved to New York in 1914. As the Museum of Fine Arts paid tribute to Maurice Prendergast in the centennial exhibition of 1960, it now honors Charles Prendergast in a similar way, proud to claim him and his enchanting creations as a unique part of the artistic heritage of his native city.

As everyone knows, Charles Prendergast commenced his career as an artist-craftsman, primarily as a designer and maker of picture frames. In this discipline he exerted all his sensibility to color and texture, he explored the possibilities of incised gesso, and he became enamored of that most precious of the frame maker's materials, gold leaf. This craftsman's experience is the foundation upon which he built his unique art, the panels, chests, and screens, incised, painted, and gilded that gave scope to his extraordinary decorative gift. A glance at them reveals his artistic predilections, the source of his inspiration: the gold-ground paintings of the Italian primitives and the book illustrations of the Persian miniaturists, the landscapes and gardens dotted with gay costumes and graceful animals that illuminate the sagas of old Persia were the dream world of Charles Prendergast which he turned into a pictorial poetry entirely his own. To it he brought a precious naïveté which forbids one ever to suspect the genuineness of his feeling.

It is impossible to dissociate the art of Charles Prendergast from that of his older brother, Maurice. And that is as it should be, for no two brothers could have been more alike in temperament nor more closely bound by mutual affection. By the same token, it is not surprising that in their art both men were inspired by the same emotion and guided by the same instinct – a simple and uninhibited love of beauty and incorruptible taste. These factors are implicit in the work of the two brothers, and they are at the root of the resemblance between them. Collaboration was inevitable and when it happened a happier marriage of style – of form and color – could hardly be imagined. The exhibition provides several examples of frame and picture where the craft and sensibility of both artists combine and interact as a perfect ensemble.

Our own collection of the work of Charles Prendergast began with the bequest of    9 a panel from John T. Spaulding in 1948. Since then we have added an important mosaic, one of his finest chests and, as the generous gift of Mrs. Charles Prendergast, a very beautiful decorative panel, *The Fountain*. Together with important frames already in the collection, the art of Charles Prendergast in its numerous forms begins to assume significant representation in the Boston Museum.

With this exhibition, a serious effort has been made for the first time to appraise the art of Charles Prendergast in all its aspects and apart from the accomplishments of his brother. In our enterprise we are fortunate to have had the collaboration of the Rutgers University Art Gallery, New Brunswick, New Jersey, and its director, Richard J. Wattenmaker, and The Phillips Collection, Washington, D. C., and its director, Mrs. Duncan Phillips, the former representing a relatively new interest in the artist, the latter an enthusiasm of many years.

PERRY T. RATHBONE
*Director*

*Museum of Fine Arts*
*Boston*
*June 1968*

## The Art of Charles Prendergast

CHARLES PRENDERGAST stands as a master among the artist-craftsmen of the ages. His self-styled medium of expression sets him apart from the other artists of his generation, but his unique, innovational creativity and the supreme merit of his aesthetic achievement most surely earn him an important place in the history of American art. The relatively limited number of objects he produced, their fragility, and the fact that most of them belong to private collections have made his work somewhat unavailable for wide public circulation. The current exhibition is, indeed, the first comprehensive presentation of his art and, as such, is long overdue this man whose singular vision so generously enriches our artistic heritage.

Charles Prendergast was born in Boston on May 27, 1863, less than four years after his now famous brother, Maurice. The brothers were exceptionally close, living and working together for most of their lives, and Maurice's intense ambition to be a painter, his intelligent and active interest in the old and modern traditions of art, and his uncompromising artistic independence no doubt furnished a rich and persuasive environment for the younger Prendergast. Charles attended Rice Grammar School and, upon graduation, took a job as errand boy at the Doll and Richards fine arts shop in Boston. One summer in the mid-eighteen-eighties, he worked his way to England on a cattle boat, returning the next year accompanied by Maurice, with whom he also visited Wales and possibly Paris. Thereafter, he briefly pursued the profession of traveling salesman of household objects, followed by a profitable but unsatisfying venture in custom woodworking. Irresolute and discontented, Charles was easily persuaded by Maurice and a friend, the painter Herman Dudley Murphy, to forsake such restrictive carpentry work for framemaking, and in 1895 in Boston he began his career in art.

Although not formally educated, Charles was by no means lacking in knowledge of the wealth of traditions of art. In 1898 and again in 1911–12, he joined Maurice in Italy to study in the museums and churches of Venice, Florence, Pisa, Siena, and probably Orvieto and Ravenna as well. Of these places Venice held a special appeal for him, both for the abundant richness of its art and for the exotic, otherworldly charm of the city itself – qualities which he was later to rephrase and give new meaning to in the substance of his work. During these trips and also at home, he sought out old frames to rework or to use as models for his own creative departures. Both brothers kept closely in touch with the current trends in French art, where so much of revolutionary importance was happening. While living in Boston, Charles availed himself of the collection of Mrs. Gardner and the Oriental and Near Eastern collections in the Museum of Fine Arts. The Prendergasts visited New York as often as possible, establishing close relationships with the members of the group later to become known as The Eight. Thus was Charles intimately associated with the two major events of early twentieth century American art – the 1908 exhibition held at the Macbeth Gallery of The Eight and the 1913 Armory Show, for which incidentally he provided a number of frames.

While it was no doubt inevitable that Charles could not content himself with frame-making forever, his first gesso panel, *Rising Sun* (Cat. no. 1), was not undertaken until 1912, when the artist was nearly fifty years of age. In October of 1914, the brothers moved to New York, and here Charles pursued his experiments with incised gesso panels in earnest. Their third floor apartment-studio at 50 Washington Square South was above the studio of their friend William Glackens; Glackens' son, Ira, later recalled the surroundings in which the Prendergasts worked:

> . . . Charles had his workbench in the backroom, where he made his . . . panels and chests. . . . The place was furnished with the minimum necessities of life, but all about hung Maurice's paintings and Charles' panels. One of Charles's . . . carved chests [see *Carved and Decorated Chest,* Cat. no. 52] stood between the two front windows. These treasures, in all their glowing colors, made the place as rich as a palace.
>
> The Prendergasts owned two . . . old Persian pottery jars in which they kept a few scraps of old brocade . . . which they had picked up in Italy . . . A group of little Italian marionettes hung by their wires in a corner of the room . . . Under a bench was a small wooden box containing ancient pieces of mosaic, . . . a treasure likewise found in Italy . . . The Prendergasts' studio, . . . as remembered by a small boy, was a magic place.[1]

In these early years of his career, Charles' work gained the admiration of a small but important group of collectors. John Quinn acquired five gesso panels.[2] Miss Lillie

1. Ira Glackens, *William Glackens and the Ashcan Group,* First Edition, Crown Publishers, Inc., 1957, pp. 116–117.
2. Quinn's panels included *Dancer and Black Stag, Head, Nude Figures, Stags Feeding,* and *Dancer and Stag.* These were sold at auction in 1927, and their whereabouts is now unknown. See *Cata-*

P. Bliss, one of the founders of the Museum of Modern Art, New York, also bought a number of panels; in addition, she commissioned Charles to make a chest (Cat. no. 52), to do decorative paneling[3] and woodwork for her music room, and to design a panel[4] (Cat. no. 12) to be hung over a mantel in the Bliss house in New York. Dr. Albert C. Barnes purchased four panels[5] and one sculpture, as well as commissioning a large number of frames for the famous collection of paintings at The Barnes Foundation in Merion, Pennsylvania; indeed, the frames done for The Barnes Foundation represent as diverse and comprehensive a selection of this aspect of Prendergast's work as can be found anywhere.

Although he tended to shy away from the limelight, Charles was at this time receiving some attention from the galleries. A 1915 group show at the Montross Gallery included six of his panels; one panel[6] and an original drawing were illustrated in the catalogue. In 1917 and 1918 he exhibited panels in the first two shows presented by the Society of Independent Artists. Charles was elected vice-president of the Society in 1917. His work also appeared at the Daniel Galleries in 1918. In 1919 an article was published in *Country Life in America* in which five of his panels and the Bliss chest were illustrated. He contributed five panels to a group show at the Montross Gallery in 1920, and in 1921 he shared an exhibition with Maurice at the Joseph Brummer Galleries, showing eight panels and one chest. In the early twenties, however, Maurice's health began to fail, and the brothers gradually retired from their public activities.

Maurice's death on February 1, 1924, marked the end of an era for Charles. He was now sixty years old, alone, and profoundly sorrowed by the loss of his closest companion and, in great measure, his primary inspiration. In 1925, during a trip to France, he married Eugénie van Kemmel. Returning to America, they settled in Westport, Con-

*logue of the John Quinn Collection,* Joseph L. Brummer and E. Weyhe, Pigeon Hill Press, Huntington, N.Y., 1926. See also *The John Quinn Collection, Sale Catalogue,* American Art Association, New York, 1927.

3. Unfortunately, this paneling, made in conjunction with painted murals by Arthur B. Davies, no longer exists.
4. This panel, the largest ever undertaken by Charles, is the only known work on which Maurice Prendergast acknowledged his collaboration by signature.
5. Two of the panels in the collection of The Barnes Foundation are illustrated in Albert C. Barnes, *The Art in Painting,* First Edition, The Barnes Foundation Press, Merion, Pennsylvania, 1925, p. 467, and Forbes Watson, "The Barnes Foundation Pt. II," *The Arts,* Vol. III, no. 2, February, 1923, p. 149.
6. Now lost.

necticut, where, with the exception of two trips to France in 1927 and 1929 and two winters in Florida in the mid-forties, Charles worked until his death in 1948 at the age of eighty-five.

Shortly after Maurice's death, Charles began his gallery affiliation with John Kraushaar. One-man shows of his work were presented at the Kraushaar Galleries in 1935, 1937, 1941, and 1947; a memorial exhibition comprised of forty works was held there in 1954. Through Kraushaar, Duncan Phillips acquired in 1926 the largest of Charles' three screens (Cat. no. 51) for his private collection. Many other private collectors sought his work, as well as such museums as the Addison Gallery of American Art (Cat. nos. 4 & 21), the Newark Museum (Cat. no. 6), and the Whitney Museum of American Art (Cat. no. 39). Altogether Charles produced about one hundred and twenty-five panels; he estimated that he carved approximately four hundred frames; he made three chests, three screens, a number of small boxes and sculptures, and one three-legged stool; in addition, he produced a number of watercolors and glass and mirror paintings.

Descriptions of Charles Prendergast by those who knew him convey the impression of a quiet, introspective man who none the less radiated a sparkling aliveness. The meticulous demands of the medium he chose served to draw out rather than subdue his creative energies, and the intense pleasure he apparently took in all aspects of craftsmanship comes through in the magical sense of delicacy and perfection of the finished surfaces. M. D. C. Crawford's account of the intricate procedure and the care with which he carried his ideas through their physical stages of development illustrates Charles' passionate thoroughness:

> . . . The character of the wood, its preparation, the mixing of glues and sizes and plasters, the grinding and mixing of colors, and the proper time and manner of applying gold and silver leaf, are all matters of deep interest [to Charles]. The method employed by Mr. Prendergast in making these panels differs somewhat from the tradition. It is more than merely a flat painting and gilding on plaster. The wood he uses is the sugar pine, or, where possible to procure, fine old white pine. On the surface the outline of his cartoon is transferred with charcoal, and the deeper lines are incised with gouges and chisels. Over this is spread several coats of gesso plaster, and while this is still wet, the more delicate lines are traced with a fine steel point [see photo of the artist at work, ca. 1918, frontispiece]. Over such figures and

14

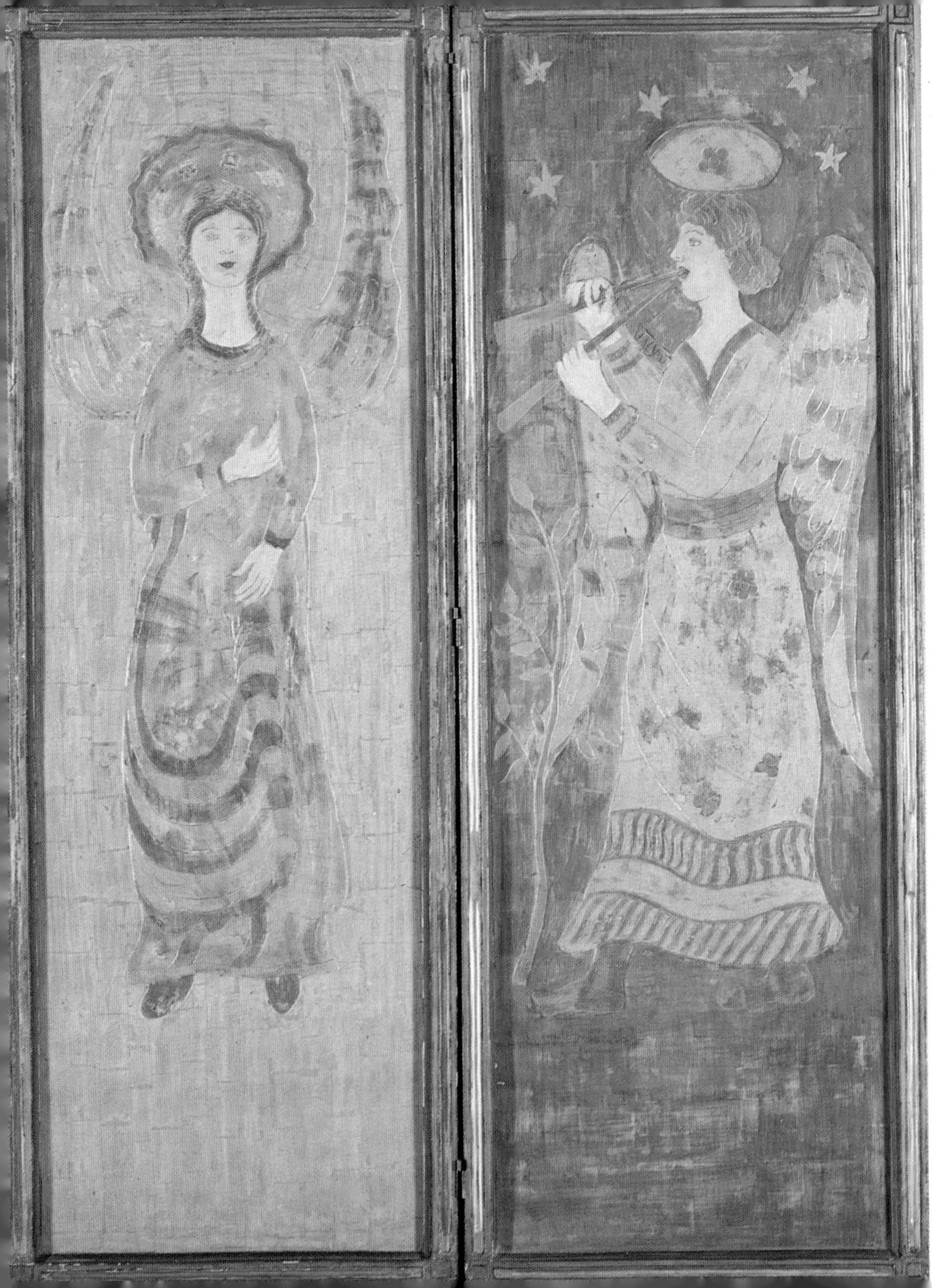

**51** SCREEN, 1916–17

details as are to be gilded is spread a second coat of special plaster. And when all this has been thoroughly dried and all roughness removed by sandpaper and pumice stone, it is ready for the application of gold and silver leaf and color...[7]

And when, in an article by Hamilton Basso, we encounter him at work on the most subtle and exacting phase of the whole undertaking, we are given to feel an ardent spirit infusing life into the raw materials of his art:

Of the many steps involved in the elaborate task of executing a panel, the most delicate and dramatic is the last – the application of the gold leaf. After tracing the picture on the gesso, softening the gesso by dipping a brush in water and moistening the surface, incising it ... and painting whatever parts of it call for paint, he is ready to tackle the gold leaf ... The gold leaf Prendergast uses, ... of eight- or ten-carat gold, is put up in twenty-five-page books, ... one sheet of gold leaf between each two pages. Few things look as innocent as these sheets of gold leaf ... Before a sheet ... is applied ... it must be removed from the book and placed on ... a gilder's cushion. Prendergast's cushion is a small, chamois-covered board, six five inches ... Prendergast approaches a sheet of gold leaf with some caution ... he opens a book ... holds it between his mouth and the cushion, purses his lips, and emits a slight puff. The sheet of gold leaf rises from its page and falls, twisting and turning in the air like a piece of half-solidified sunlight, to the cushion. Not flat, though. Prendergast warily takes up his gilder's knife ... and with it lifts the gold leaf. Then he suddenly jerks the knife from under the gold leaf ... and emits another puff ... It lies flat on the cushion ... He picks up his knife with his right hand, slices a piece of gold leaf from the sheet, and deftly lifts it from the cushion with the blade. Then, with his left hand, he reaches for a brush – or what the gilding trade calls a tip – made of a layer of camel's hair glued between two layers of cardboard that form a handle. Keeping one eye on the bit of gold leaf trembling on the knife blade, he runs the hair of the tip across his own hair, then gingerly ... transfers it [the bit of gold leaf] to the gesso. The natural oils of the hair, gilders have discovered, tend to make the gold leaf cling to the tip, and this facilitates handling. Prendergast's strange and ambidextrous performance, which most nearly resembles that of a harried man simultaneously slicing bread and brushing his hair, is repeated over and over again.[8]

With such vitality Prendergast reaches into and objectifies for us his own responsiveness to the world around him. The general purpose of all artistic expression is to embody in a new and personal form the qualities by which the matters-of-fact of existence become matters-of-importance to us, and the creative artist is he who is able

7. See Bibliography.    8. See Bibliography.                                                          17

**3** CALLING OF SS. PETER AND ANDREW, circa 1914

to penetrate to the essence of what *he* deems important, what interests *him* in the objective world, and to convey to us what he alone, by virtue of his individuality, has found. This he does by way of a medium chosen because of the values, or qualities, especially belonging to its expressive province. In Prendergast's case, the interest quite clearly belongs to the decorative value of things specifically expressed in terms of the sensuous appeal of color and an ornamental resplendence of linear rhythms. These are enclosed in a wealth of pictorial relationships which draw upon our potential knowledge of such values and which expand, by the uniqueness of their presentation, our understanding of them. His selection of the difficult and limited gesso-ground medium in which to work his ideas reflects a particular enjoyment in the careful shaping of his vision, for the medium itself exercises a significant degree of influence over the effects achieved. Thus, for example, the making of a line by incising or carving may tend to result in a rigidity, which Prendergast uses to strengthen the quality of animated terseness that his line, by his own predisposition, possesses; and, too, the gesso surface itself demands sureness of plan and deft clarity of color application, both of which are, under Prendergast's sensitive hand, instrumental to the distinct character of his art; the very density and weight of the medium are made to contribute a reassuring solidity to the delicate handling of line and color. The ability to make expressive use of the natural tendencies of a technically demanding medium is, of course, the essence of the artist-craftsman and should be recognized as an inseparable feature of Prendergast's vision.

Prendergast's early work in framemaking, though by no means representative of the scope and subtlety of his entire achievement, already pointed the way to what was to be characteristic of his principal statement of interest. In the frames too we see his savoring of the exotic luxuriousness of gold, but a gold that has been restrained and naturalized in reflective brilliance and quieted in hue – that is to say, a gold which has been played out equally for its color and its lustrous sheen. In the frames too we see a susceptibility to the appeal of gentle, pervasive patterning, stated in his own terms of a pert, delicately terse line, a lively stippling, a springy, rhythmically continuous banding, and a textural solidity and weight, all of which, when illustratively allied to the world of fact, says also such things that grace existence as flowers, leaves, or, perhaps, Florentine metal work. In addition, the frames show a keen sense for the fittingness of the internal patterning to the dimensions of the decorated surface, finesse in using that patterning to determine, in part, the sense of scale of the whole, and an extraordinary ability to order the elements of his design to make of the whole a simple, one-piece entity, however profusely the elements may abound within. And finally, his technical mastery comes through to lend a distinct joyousness to the created object.

These general characteristics found in the frames crystalize in Prendergast's definitive work – the panels, screens, chests, and sculptures. The means of color and line, freed to answer solely to his decorative purposes, flower out in a never-ending series of relationships through which the ideas that interested him are explored to the utmost: the lustrous gold color becomes mingled with and set against deep or clear or gently muted blues, fresh and varied shades of green, delicate, exotic purples and reds, crisp yellows and oranges, whites that sing out with a startling vibrancy, all ordered in such a way that they not only convey their own color identities but serve also to realize a rich, saturating colorfulness, within which each individual color seems to have reached the pinnacle of its sensuous value. The terse, animated line, too, achieves in its own fashion a full-fledged "colorfulness," as each episode of it takes on a variety of roles in the multiplicity of rhythmic themes that pervade his work: quick, profusely evident staccato beats play among long, sinuously elegant phrases and gently uplifting curvilinear movements; brief arabesques, scallops, circles, stars, and flowers that fill compartments of skirt, fish, or a piece of sky or landscape bestow a piquantly static note of variety on the simple, resilient, repetitive linear themes that prevail; large and small color-filled shapes are contained by line with a subtly vivacious restraint that lends equal emphasis to the particular nature of the linear movement that surrounds and to the color statement within; and throughout the picture surfaces line threads its way, sometimes continuously and sometimes let-go and picked up again, linking figure to animal to foreground and background, or gold to blue and green and purple, across and up and down, as though the whole were a one-piece tapestry woven on a bizarrely irregular loom. Both line and color are cast into an illustrative framework that elaborates on and clarifies their decorative natures by way of those bare essentials of figure, animal, and landscape that speak as much of the exotic, the charming, the graceful, the picturesque as do the line and color themselves. Indeed, the entire illustrative presentation is so nearly at one with the qualities of line and color that it seems almost a literal translation of these means; each figure says with its total character "exquisite arabesque," each animal "taut poise," and the

21   THE HILL TOWN, 1928

out-of-doors setting provides another way of saying the light, airy charm expressed initially by the means. So that, put together like this, with the values of the illustrative and plastic aspects mutually interchangeable, the whole partakes of a naïveté and child-like directness which evokes a feeling of a fairy tale made real.

Both thematically and qualitatively, Prendergast freely adapted material from a number of the traditions of art; in fact, the traditions to which his work is related seem almost to fill the same function for his purposes as a model or landscape fills for a painter concerned with expressing his values through the things of this world. For the most part, these borrowings were made from sources which appear exotic to the western eye and which deal in the general range of the decorative effects that interested Prendergast – Persian and Hindu miniatures, Oriental art and decoration, Egyptian frescoes, bas reliefs, and gilt-wood sculptures, Greek painted vases, Etruscan frescoes, terra-cottas, and bronzes, Coptic textiles, Byzantine mosaics, and early Italian panels and frescoes. To these may be added from among the modern painters the work of Gauguin and Matisse – particularly as they too dealt with ancient and eastern decorative ideas – and of his brother, Maurice, through whom he is indirectly allied to countless artists, from the Venetians to Cézanne, whose interests were not confined to decorative effects.

Persian and Hindu miniatures provide the most direct and conspicuous influence on Prendergast's work. From them, most noticeably, he takes over an abundance of illustrative material – actually, almost his entire population of flattened, tersely delineated birds, deer, fishes, costumed dancing girls, horseback riders, as well as the foliaged landscapes and mountainous backgrounds – all of which, though easily recognizable as Persian or Hindu in origin, has been fully reinterpreted for his purposes. While in the sources the illustrative subjects appear as rigid, stereotyped, somewhat indifferent vehicles for the decorative interplay of set linear themes, ornamental motifs, and areas of contrasting color, Prendergast endows them with a certain poignant individuality of their own that introduces a partly naturalistic, partly expressive note absent from the earlier versions: line, though terse, clean-cut, and continuous, also assumes a delicately movemented quality, such as in *Dancers* (Cat. no. 5) or the seated angel in *Decorative Composition* (Cat. no. 15), that lends a conviction and reality to the gesture portrayed; a lilting, poised grace qualifies the compartmental setness of such units as the uplifted hands and the ascending birds in *Flight of the Birds* (Cat.

**18** FAIRY STORY, circa 1920, (reworked in 1946)

no. 4) or the rearing deer in *The Hill Town* (Cat. no. 21); the sceptre-holding angel in the right panel of *Screen* (Cat. no. 51) has an ultra-fine sense of balancing of head upon neck that tells of its uniqueness; and even the facial expressions tend throughout to be less mask-like than those of the Persians or Hindus and more in keeping with the light, sprightly gaiety with which the line is tempered. In short, Prendergast adds to his illustrative borrowings a positive feeling of personality, a gentle picturesqueness that lends an expressive dimension to their decorative impact. Though these echoes of naturalism reflect to a great extent the influence of Maurice, they have very definitely come through Charles' mind and have been distilled to the decorative-expressive essence that he needed to say what was his alone to say.

Along with this illustrative assemblage comes the important and pervasive arabesque line and the profusion of decorative motifs mentioned before, both characteristic of Oriental and Near Eastern art. Somewhat like Matisse, Prendergast handles the arabesque in a variety of ways: on occasion it is rendered with a pure Eastern or Hindu fluidity (see the branches in *Donkey Rider*, Cat. no. 19); at other times it takes on an elongated, staturesque grace and firmness that is reminiscent of the more majestic drawing of Greek and Egyptian art (see standing figures in *Calling of SS. Peter and Andrew*, Cat. no. 3); sometimes it has the fine, hard precision of the Persians (see the deer and horses in *The Riders*, Cat. no. 7) and, at others, the rugged, often banding effect found in Byzantine mosaics that Matisse also shares in (as throughout the bottom area of *Screen*, Cat. no. 51, and others). The profusion of decorative motifs echoes the let-go of the arabesque. Prendergast's tendency to give these motifs free play over the entire picture surface (e.g., *Fairy Story*, Cat. no. 18, *Golden Fantasy*, Cat. no. 20, *Play, International House*, Cat. no. 23) is suggestive of some Persian miniatures and of Coptic textiles and helps to express a similar one-pieceness of picture surface. Unlike the Persian and Coptic usage, however, and partly because of the incised-gesso technique, these motifs seem to enter into the substance of the objects they decorate, at once securely fixing in its place each area in which they occur and enhancing its solidity. In *Rising Sun* (Cat. no. 1), for example, the stiff, incised scalloping of the wings and pineapple-like trees emphasizes both their substantiality and location in order to achieve the weighty, static, three-beat drama of these areas against the complex arabesque arrangement of the deer-angel unit; similarly, the deer takes on a positive identity and weight sufficient to stand up against that of the wings and trees by way of the circles inscribed on its back. Such plastic use of the decorative motifs is characteristic of Prendergast's work in general and occurs with a remarkable variety of effects according to each picture design.

From the Persians, too, Prendergast adopts many of his compositional features, especially the overlapped groupings of figures in front of and sandwiched between flat, mound-like units (e. g., *The Riders,* Cat. no. 7, *Screen,* Cat. no. 51, and many others), and the top-to-bottom layered spatial distortion in which perspective takes the form of an elevation of the background. In Prendergast's treatment, however, the modulated appearance of color and variation of line impart a subtly atmospheric space to this relatively flat scheme. To these borrowings he adds the scale and the at-the-front-of-the-surface placement of the 14th century Italian panel and fresco painters, features he clearly incorporates into the full length figures on the back of *Screen* (Cat. no. 51) but occurring in solution throughout (e. g., *Madonna and Child,* Cat. no. 2, and *The Offering,* Cat. no. 8); both these – the scale and frontality – contribute a near-at-hand quality, quite different from the miniature remoteness of the Persian scenes, that reinforces the picturesque naturalism conveyed by his handling of the subjects and space. The Oriental traditions, too, make a large contribution to his compositional ideas. For one thing, his use of arbitrary variations of scale as a pictorial device demonstrates the same feel for the unexpected, as, for example, in *Screen* (Cat. no. 51), where the two large women midway down the left panel provide a daring and imaginative surprise element, as do, also the three elongated figures behind the donkey rider at the left of *Decorative Composition* (Cat. no. 15). Note might be made, in this context, of the frequent decorative use of a monogram reminiscent of the Japanese-Chinese *cartouche.* Bizarre shapes of an oriental cast serve as other surprise elements within the compositions, such as may be seen in the background areas and the sail in *Calling of SS. Peter and Andrew* (Cat. no. 3) and the mountain ranges in *Flight of the Birds* (Cat. no. 4), *The Hill Town* (Cat. no. 21), *Screen* (Cat. no. 51), and others. These hint at the influence of Gauguin as well, as the Oriental fineness is tempered by a rugged irregularity and massiveness. In some of the panels, such as *The Hill Town* (Cat. no. 21) and *Play, International House* (Cat. no. 23), among others, composition takes the form of distinct horizontal bands broken up into a series of internally patterned areas. But while the Oriental version of this type of organization consists of a careful balancing of plain areas against patterned ones, in Prendergast's work it serves as a stabilizing device that allows for an unbelievable abundance of decorative motifs and illustrative elements to saturate the surface area – different-sized rectangular shapes, extended wavy lines, small scallops ornamenting trees and rosette-like flowers, criss-crosses, hatchings, combined with horses, figures, birds, boats, deer, dogs, to name a few. Altogether, the effect is one of a panoramic grandeur quite different from the *intime* bizarrerie of the East. Another compositional idea Prendergast makes frequent use of is that of the Greek-Egyptian-Byzantine frieze; obvious examples of this include *Decorative Composition* (Cat. no. 15) and *The Fountain* (Cat. no. 22), but it can also be found in subsidiary areas of other panels, such as *Flight of the Birds* (Cat. no. 4) and *Dancers* (Cat. no. 5); and throughout his work the near-at-hand feeling of figures or foliage filling the front of the picture surface reflects this influence along with that of the Italian frescoes and panels mentioned before.

The use of gold leaf is common to the Oriental, Near Eastern, Egyptian, Byzantine, and early Italian traditions which Prendergast adapted, but nowhere else can it be found to possess the positive sense of being *color* as well as gold that it does in his work. Toned down in reflectiveness to a subtle, lost-and-found gleam, mellowed to a pale, delicately modulated hue, and worked into the substance of the other colors of his palette, it becomes one with a rich color presentation which, in general, combines the clarity of the Persians with the muted quality of the Italians and the purity, simplicity, and naturalness of Maurice. From the Orient and Near East he borrows the delicate, somewhat purplish reds and lavenders that pervade his work, but such exotic hues rarely set the color tone of a picture. In application, he tends to follow the Oriental practice of irregularly brushed on color patches or areas that give a light-filled watercolor effect to the surface. As in Maurice's work, seldom do color areas juxtapose each other simply as dark-light contrast, but seem to follow each upon the other in a pageant-like succession that binds the surface together. Although most like Maurice in the quality of colorfulness he achieves at his best, Charles' color partakes of a particular delicacy and purity that evolves from his sensitive handling of the gesso ground and gold leaf. Thus, for example, while his work is marked by an absence of shadowing – a characteristic found both in Maurice's work and in Egyptian and Near Eastern Art – he uses the medium to achieve that enhancement of color which light-shadow embellishment may give; for, the very existence of an incised line or bas-relief structure results in the casting of varying shadows that, in turn, make an intriguing play with the subtle quality of light given off by the transient emergence of the gesso ground from beneath the color and the ephemeral gleam of the gold leaf – transforming his color effects into something singularly rich and personal and not at all his sources. His uniqueness is perhaps best exemplified by the intense color quality in their picture contexts of his bare-gesso whites, an effect unequaled anywhere else in the traditions.

By far the most pervasive influence on Prendergast was the work of his brother, Maurice. The profound intimacy of ideas between the two is freely reflected in the joyous spontaneity and jewel-like, color-laden decorativeness which permeate both their work, as well as the innovational flexibility with which each handles his chosen medium. In addition to the similarity of color already mentioned, Charles' tendency to minimize the distinction between background and foreground and to give all areas of the picture equal importance, his front-of-the-surface treatment of subject, his use of a general horizontal movement across the surface by way of color areas to knit the picture together, his gentle naturalism all have their parallel in Maurice's painting. Despite their kinship, however, Charles was fully involved in his own particular vision, as may be seen in his strong, almost exclusive, attraction to the exotic traditions of the past and his interest in the full-fledged illustrative nature of his subjects. Indeed, the very craftsmanship which was so much a part of Charles' makeup indicated a decorative orientation unlike Maurice's, for the effects achieved – of which the exotic richness of the gold leaf, the rhythmic linear structure of the incising, the very weight and texture of the surfaces themselves are a part – stem from Charles' personal and creative exploration of the potential of the medium in which he chose to work.

Prendergast's sculptures – woodcarvings with gold leaf – are as natural an extension of his framemaking as the gesso panels. Woodcarving or whittling is a venerable tradition in America, and not since the early New Mexican carver of *bultos* and the painted woodcarvings of the itinerant Pennsylvania artist-craftsman Wilhelm Schimmel have there been small scale sculptures of such considerable expressive stature on the American scene. These sculptures are characterized by a firmness of surface enhanced in its three-dimensional density by the application of red ground and gold leaf which highlight the crisply faceted carving; in addition, they convey an illustrative presence through expressive stances and convincing gestures. Again, as in the panels, exotic traditions are brought into play. *Eve* (Cat. no. 57), a dignified and regal figure, seems

to recall the gilt-wood figures of the Egyptians, with the subsidiary bird unit having a distinctly Near Eastern source. The figure expresses a small-scale power and solidity, and the vigorous quality of the whole is amplified rather than reduced by the gilt and by the incised details which add variety to the basic mass. *Man Dancing* (Cat. no. 60) recalls in its caught fixity of stance the Etruscan terra-cotta figures and small bronze sculptures. Decorative values, while inherent in the gilding and the movemented silhouette, are not here sacrificed to the expressiveness of the carving. The pose suggests the frieze motif in three dimensions. *Angel* (Cat. no. 58) is more static in gesture and suggests Prendergast's link to the early Italian Renaissance. *Kneeling Figure* (Cat. no. 61) is reminiscent of early Egyptian and Roman sculpture in its pose, and its smooth surface and luxuriantly incised base combine to heighten an overall richness. The later woodcarvings of animals, such as *Dolphin* (Cat. no. 62), are more sleek of surface and immediately decorative. Taken as a whole, these sculptures are vigorous, sure, direct, and fully three-dimensional.

In summary, Prendergast's kinship with the traditions of art is based on a natural affinity for the decorative ideas they have disclosed. He is neither imitative nor affected in his approach to them, and the numerous traditional borrowings he makes are at all times made to serve his own original ideas.

Prendergast's entire body of work tends to divide into three general phases which are distinguishable both on the basis of differences of emphasis in decorative interests and by shifts in the predominance of traditional influences. Loosely, these phases include, as Prendergast himself named them, the Oriental or "Celestial" (*ca.* 1912–28), the Transitional (*ca.* 1928–35), and the Modern (*ca.* 1935–48).

The earliest of these is marked by a highly experimental approach to the medium and reaches the richest and most varied expression of Prendergast's pictorial values. In general, the multitude of traditional borrowings mentioned above are thoroughly in solution and are dominated by his own gentle naturalism and decorative interests. The panels themselves encompass a diversity of effects, from the weightily dramatic simplicity of the sculptured *Rising Sun* (Cat. no. 1) to the exquisite complexity of *Screen* (Cat. no. 51), from the poised fixity of *The Riders* (Cat. no. 7) to the movemented grace of *Dancers* (Cat. no. 5), from the formal presentation of *Madonna and Child* (Cat. no. 2) to the piquantly off-beat balancing of *Calling of SS. Peter and Andrew* (Cat. no. 3) or the almost intimate sense of portraiture of *The Offering* (Cat. no. 8). Although the

works of the first phase show a gradual development towards a flatter, more directly decorative effect and a giving way of the Byzantine influence to the Greek and Coptic, there is a consistency of expressive purpose that pervades the whole period. Color, enhanced by a lavish use of gold, saturates the entire surfaces of these panels and is equally distributed over the major and minor illustrative units and background areas for the achievement of that colorfulness which Prendergast has contributed to the tradition of art. The illustrative matter is invariably exotic in character and is qualified by a front-of-the-surface bigness. Subtle and atmospheric episodes of space move delicately between the frontal units as they are needed to ease the way for the abundance of decorative motifs and large, freely articulated shapes. Line in this early work tends to be played out for its long, curvilinear sensuousness and gathers together all elements in a spirited uplifting motion. And throughout, each of the components seems in context just rightly chosen to serve the idea of a given panel, giving rise to a sense of perfection that is the psychological equivalent of the line and color cohesiveness and the compositional balance within the picture surface.

In the work of the middle and late periods, there is a distinctly further lessening of the Byzantine, Greek, Egyptian, and Italian influences and a concurrent coming to the fore of the Persian idea of miniature and the set, somewhat staccato-like, compositional themes found in Oriental art. The long linear sweeps that united the early work give way to a more static play of compartmental areas against each other; in the middle phase, this tends to occur in terms of decorative clusters, and in the late, by the isolation of areas. The illustrative aspect assumes more importance in its own right and gradually relinquishes its exotic other-worldliness for the naturalism of contemporary material. Indeed, by the late phase, these themes are drawn almost exclusively from everyday life – fairs, polo games, circuses, etc. – although they retain in handling an Oriental-Persian character. At the same time, however, color themes become less naturalistic and take on an Oriental flavor of a contrasting interplay within a limited range of hues; especially in the last period, the color simplification is directed towards the light gaiety and pert drama of rhythmically interspersed and recurrent color units, such as we see in the ordered repetition of pinks, oranges, purples, and greens among the figures in *Polo Players No. 1* (Cat. no. 46). In the Transitional and Modern periods figures and other units tend to be silhouetted against background areas rather than

linearly and colorfully at one with them; decorative motifs are similarly isolated, con-

**16** POLO PLAYERS No. 1, circa 1941

veying a sense of detail that helps to emphasize the miniature effect. In the middle period such isolation occurs largely by way of the static quality of the incising and the compositional division of the surface into bands, squares, and rectangles, while the late work achieves it by the compartmental separation of color units. Space in both phases becomes more a matter of linear perspective, as in *Play, International House* (Cat. no. 23), or of a decrease in size of units as they are placed closer to the top of the picture surface, as in *The Hill Town* (Cat. no. 21), *The Fountain* (Cat. no. 22), or *North Shore* (Cat. no. 38). These general differences are clearly indicated by a comparison, simply on the basis of their illustrative natures, of *Decorative Composition* (Cat. no. 15) of 1918 with *The Fountain* (Cat. no. 22) of 1930, since the latter is evidently a re-working of the earlier scheme. In the former, the illustrative ideas are altogether sub-merged into the sedate, gently monumental, frieze-like continuity of surface; such illustrative specificity that accrues to the figures or animals does so in terms of the linear and color variety among them and is meaningful because of the particular ex-pressive idea each unit embodies; it is the delicate poise of the standing figure in a toga, the lilting sense of balance of the man running at the left, the piquant "seated-ness" of the center angel, and so on, that the illustrative facts present. In the latter, however, the facts present a pipe player, a running man, a woman holding a tray, all told with the same static line that emphasizes the compartmental isolation of areas, the miniature orientation, and the staid organization characteristic of this phase. In the last period, the general tendencies are modified also by an almost total absence of the ornamental motifs and an increased gentleness of line and color for the accom-plishment of the lightweight color drama that pervades these works. Occasionally, one finds in this period pictures frankly derivative of Maurice, for example *Bathers Under the Trees* (Cat. no. 44) and *Bathers* (Cat. no. 45), but in such works as *Polo Players No. 2* (Cat. no. 47) the influences, largely Persian and Oriental, are thoroughly absorbed into Prendergast's own form.

With the sureness of a craftsman, nowhere in his work did Prendergast linger over effects irrelevant to his view of reality. The means by which he articulates his vision – principally color and line – are always handled simply and directly to the purpose of his interests. It is not the flexibility of line to draw upon a wealth of values that he explores nor the full expressive potential of color; he does not, for example, seek

**53** CARVED AND DECORATED CHEST, 1926–27

66  MOSAIC, circa 1916–18

through his means to portray all the warmth and power and depth and richness of the things of our world that interested a Renoir or a Titian. His line is terse, tending to the curvilinear, and gently restrained; his color, always first of all itself as a sensuous entity and important mainly on that account. What he does do, with all the selective instinct of a highly creative artist, is to draw out the full decorative potential of the line and color that are his by the vast array of fanciful and picturesque contexts which make up the world of his "heart's desire." The whole of his work becomes an innocent dream, rich in all those things that we associate with grace and charm and exotic felicity. He shows us, as with a magic wand, a world redolently aglow with sultan's gems and nature's abundance, bathed in the mellow light of a myriad of golden suns, a world of enchanted life timed to dance to some gentle, linear song of delicately taut, rhyming arabesques and dainty grace notes, a world, indeed, where the exquisitely strange is the natural and where laid out before us is all the hushed opulence of those magical delights which may please the unspoiled, serenely receptive senses.

RICHARD J. WATTENMAKER
*Hockessin*                    *Director*
*June, 1968*                   *Rutgers University Art Gallery*

## Selected Bibliography

CRAWFORD, M.D.C.  "The Carved Gesso Panels of Charles E. Prendergast." *Country Life in America,* Vol. XXXVI, No. 5, September, 1919, pp. 47–49.

PACH, WALTER  "The Wizard Wood-Carver." *Shadowland,* Vol. VIII, No. 3, May, 1923, pp. 10–11, 72.

BROOKS, VAN WYCK  "Anecdotes of Maurice Prendergast," pp. 33–45; "Charles Prendergast," pp. 46–47, in *The Prendergasts,* Retrospective Exhibition of the Work of Maurice and Charles Prendergast, Addison Gallery of American Art, Phillips Academy, Andover Massachusetts, October, 1938.

SAWYER, CHARLES H.  "The Prendergasts." *Parnassus,* Vol. X, No. 5, October, 1938, pp. 9–11.

BASSO, HAMILTON  "A Glimpse of Heaven." *New Yorker,* Vol. XXII, No. 24, July 27, 1946, pp. 24–30; No. 25, August 3, 1946, pp. 28–37.

RHYS, HEDLEY HOWELL  "Maurice Prendergast." Museum of Fine Arts, Boston and Harvard University Press, Cambridge, 1960.

## Selected Exhibitions

1915    *Montross Gallery:* six carved panels. Group show including Maurice Prendergast, William Glackens, Arthur B. Davies, Walt Kuhn, Charles Sheeler, Man Ray, and others.

1917    *Bourgeois Gallery:* two panels, *Decorative Panel No. 1* and *Decorative Panel No. 2.* Group show including Maurice Prendergast, William Glackens, and John Marin.

1917    *Society of Independent Artists:* one panel, catalogue no. 106

1918    *Society of Independent Artists:* one panel, catalogue no. 604.

1920    *Montross Gallery*: five panels. Group show including Maurice Prendergast, William Glackens, Arthur B. Davies, Robert Henri, and Marsden Hartley.

1921    *Joseph Brummer Galleries; Exhibition of Works by Maurice B. Prendergast and Charles E. Prendergast*: eight panels and one chest, catalogue nos. 38–46.

1926    *John Quinn Collection Memorial Exhibition*: one panel, *Dancer and Stags,* catalogue no. 6.

1929    *The Harvard Society for Contemporary Art*

1931    *Museum of Modern Art; Lizzie P. Bliss Memorial Exhibition:* one panel, *Men and Deer,* catalogue no. 112, illustrated.

1935    *Kraushaar Galleries:* first one-man exhibition; nineteen panels, one screen, one painting on glass, and watercolors.

1937    *Kraushaar Galleries:* second one-man exhibition; thirteen panels, one screen, and one mirror.

1938    *Addison Gallery of American Art; The Prendergasts*: nineteen panels, one chest and two screens.

1941    *Kraushaar Galleries:* third one-man exhibition.

1947    *Kraushaar Galleries:* fourth one-man exhibition; twenty-one panels.

1954    *Kraushaar Galleries Memorial Exhibition*: thirty-two panels, one screen, one chest, and six woodcarvings.

1963    *Davis Galleries:* twenty-eight watercolors, three panels, and three woodcarvings.    39

40

# Catalogue of the Exhibition

All works are listed by type of object in chronological order. Date given where known. Height precedes width. All dimensions given in inches. The panels consist of: gessoed wood or, occasionally, masonite or composition board – carved and/or incised; tempera or watercolor or both; gold leaf and/or, rarely, silver leaf.

## Panels

1   RISING SUN, 1912.
    $12 \times 17^3/_4$
    Signed lower right: C. P.
    Lent by Mrs. Charles Prendergast
    (Color plate, p. 8)

2   MADONNA AND CHILD, circa 1912–13.
    $17^1/_2 \times 12^1/_2$
    Unsigned
    Lent by Mrs. Charles Prendergast

3   CALLING OF SS. PETER AND ANDREW, circa 1914.
    $23 \times 31$
    Signed upper left: monogram C. P.
    An adaptation of the mosaic, *Calling of SS. Peter and Andrew,* in the church of
    S. Apollinare Nuovo in Ravenna. Illustrated in *Country Life in America,*
    September, 1919, in an unfinished state by an early photograph of the panel
    (see bibliography) and incorrectly titled *Miracle of the Fishes.*
    Lent by Tecosky-Schuchar Associates
    (Color plate, p. 18)

4   FLIGHT OF THE BIRDS, circa 1915.
    23 x 31
    Signed lower left: Charles Prendergast
    Lent by Addison Gallery of American Art
    Gift of Mr. Thomas Cochran

5   DANCERS, circa 1915.
    23 x 31
    Signed lower left: C. Prendergast
    Lent by Mrs. Charles Prendergast

6   FIGURES, circa 1916–17.
    $27^3/_4 \times 22^1/_2$
    Signed lower left: monogram C. P.
    Lent by The Newark Museum

7   THE RIDERS, circa 1916–17.
    30 x 23
    Signed lower right: C. Prendergast
    Anonymous loan

8   THE OFFERING, circa 1916–17.
    20 x 25
    Signed lower left: monogram C. P.
    Lent by Dr. John J. McDonough

9   DECORATIVE PANEL, circa 1916–17.
    $22^1/_2 \times 30^1/_2$
    Signed lower left: C. Prendergast
    Lent by Mrs. Faber Lewis

10 SUNSET, circa 1916–17.
$16^1/_2 \times 13^3/_4$
Signed lower left: C. Prendergast
Lent by Mrs. Charles Prendergast

11 THEATRE DIONYSIUS, circa 1916–17.
$12 \times 17$
Unsigned
Made as a sign for a private outdoor theater in Wayland, Massachusetts.
Anonymous loan

12 THE SPIRIT OF THE HUNT, circa 1917.
$55 \times 81^1/_2$
Signed lower left: M.
B.
P. C. P.
This panel was commissioned by Lillie Bliss and hung above the mantelpiece
in the Bliss home at 29 East 37th Street. It is the only known panel signed by both
Maurice Prendergast as well as Charles. Maurice probably painted the upper
section including most of the sky.
Lent by Mrs. Bliss Parkinson
(Boston only.)

13 DEER HUNTERS, circa 1917.
$22^3/_4 \times 30^3/_4$
Signed left center: monogram C. P.
Anonymous loan

14 FANTASY, 1917.
$20 \times 24$
Signed lower left: monogram C. P.
Lent by Mr. and Mrs. John Marin, Jr.

15    DECORATIVE COMPOSITION, 1918.
      $23^3/_4 \times 71$
      Signed lower left: Charles Prendergast
      Lent by Mr. Elliott Levin

16    BOUNDING DEER, circa 1918.
      $14 \times 19$
      Signed lower right: monogram C. P.
      Lent by Mr. Morris D. Crawford, Jr.

17    FLOWERS, circa 1919.
      $15^3/_4 \times 29$
      Unsigned
      Lent by Mrs. Thomas Spencer

18    FAIRY STORY, circa 1920 (reworked in 1946).
      $22 \times 31$
      Signed lower left: Charles Prendergast
      Formerly in the collection of William Glackens
      Lent by Mrs. Charles Prendergast
      (Color plate, p. 24)

19    DONKEY RIDER, circa 1920–25.
      $18 \times 20$
      Signed lower right: Charles Prendergast
      Anonymous loan

20    GOLDEN FANTASY, circa 1925–30.
      $16 \times 29^1/_4$
      Unsigned
      Lent by Mr. and Mrs. William Marshall Fuller

15

17

57

21  THE HILL TOWN, 1928.
    $38^{1}/_{2} \times 48^{1}/_{2}$
    Signed lower left: C. Prendergast
    Lent by Addison Gallery of American Art
    Gift of Miss Lillie P. Bliss
    (Color plate, p. 21)

22  THE FOUNTAIN, circa 1930.
    $31^{1}/_{4} \times 61^{3}/_{4}$
    Signed lower left: C. Prendergast
    Lent by the Museum of Fine Arts, Boston
    Gift of Mrs. Charles Prendergast

23  PLAY, INTERNATIONAL HOUSE, 1931.
    $44 \times 75$
    Signed and dated lower right: Charles Prendergast 1931
    Lent by International House, New York
    Gift of Mrs. John D. Rockefeller

24  HOLIDAY BEACH SCENE, circa 1931–32.
    $28^{1}/_{2} \times 59^{3}/_{4}$
    Signed lower right: Charles Prendergast
    Anonymous loan

25  MARKET DAY, 1935.
    $23^{1}/_{2} \times 32^{3}/_{4}$
    Signed lower right: Charles Prendergast
    Lent by Mrs. John W. S. Platt
    (Color plate, p. 23)

26

27

26   ZINNIAS, circa 1935.
     15 x 24
     Signed upper right: C. Prendergast
     Lent by Mr. and Mrs. Granville M. Brumbaugh

27   ZINNIAS, circa 1935.
     $13^3/_4$ x $22^1/_4$
     Unsigned
     Lent by Mr. and Mrs. Henry W. Breyer, Jr.

28   FLOWERS, circa 1935.
     $17^5/_8$ x $13^1/_2$
     Signed lower left: monogram C. P.
     Lent by the Museum of Fine Arts, Boston
     Bequest of John T. Spaulding

29   THE RIDERS, circa 1935
     24 x 36
     Signed lower left: C. Prendergast
     Lent by Mr. John Wilkie

30   BOUNDING DEER, 1936.
     15 x $19^1/_4$
     Signed lower left: C. Prendergast
     Lent by Ira and Nancy Glackens

31   COUNTRY FAIR, 1936.
     21 x 24
     Signed lower left: C. Prendergast
     Lent by Mrs. Robert M. Pennoyer

32   THE WINNER, 1936.
     $18^1/_2$ x 22
     Signed lower left: C. Prendergast
     Lent by Mr. and Mrs. Bob London

66

33 FRUIT IN A SILVER BOWL, 1936.
$19^1/_2 \times 19^3/_4$
Signed lower right: C. Prendergast
Lent by Mr. and Mrs. Henry W. Breyer, Jr.

34 FLOWER VASE, 1936.
$19^3/_4 \times 15^5/_8$
Signed lower left: monogram C. P.
Lent by The Rita and Daniel Fraad Collection
(Boston and Rutgers only.)

35 NEW ENGLAND VILLAGE, circa 1936.
$20^3/_4 \times 26^3/_4$
Signed lower left: C. Prendergast
Lent by Mrs. J. Woodward Redmond

36 RACETRACK, 1937.
$27 \times 32^1/_2$
Signed lower right: C. Prendergast
Lent by Mr. Robert F. Woolworth
(Color plate, p. 29)

37 CENTRAL PARK, 1938.
$20^1/_2 \times 15^1/_2$
Signed and dated lower left: C. Prendergast 1938
Lent by the Estate of Mrs. R. Barclay Scull

38 NORTH SHORE, 1939.
$26 \times 28$
Signed and dated lower right: C. Prendergast 1939
Lent by Mr. and Mrs. Philip F. Newman
(Color plate, p. 31)

33

35

39   NEW YORK WORLD'S FAIR 1939, 1939.
     $24 \times 27^{1}/_{2}$
     Signed and dated lower left: C. Prendergast 1939
     Lent by Whitney Museum of American Art

40   SKATERS AT THE WORLD'S FAIR, 1940.
     $30 \times 31^{1}/_{2}$
     Signed and dated lower right: C. Prendergast 1940
     Lent by Mrs. Charles Prendergast

41   CIRCUS, 1940.
     $25 \times 25$
     Signed and dated lower left: C. Prendergast 1940
     Lent by Mrs. Charles Prendergast

42   AFTER THE SHOW, circa 1940.
     $16^{3}/_{4} \times 15^{1}/_{2}$
     Signed lower right: C. Prendergast
     Lent by Mr. and Mrs. Charles H. Sawyer

43   CIRCUS RIDER No. 9, circa 1940.
     $17 \times 13$
     Signed lower right: monogram C. P.
     Lent by Mrs. Charles Prendergast

44   BATHERS UNDER THE TREES, circa 1940.
     $20^{1}/_{2} \times 26^{1}/_{2}$
     Signed lower left: C. Prendergast
     Anonymous loan

45   BATHERS, 1941.
     $26^{1}/_{4} \times 32^{1}/_{4}$
     Signed lower left: C. Prendergast
     Anonymous loan

42

45

C. PREMDERGAST

84

**47**

46   POLO PLAYERS No. 1, circa 1941.
     $20 \times 23^{1}/_{4}$
     Signed lower left: C. Prendergast
     Lent by Mrs. Charles Prendergast
     (Color plate, p. 33)

47   POLO PLAYERS No. 2, 1944.
     $23^{1}/_{2} \times 23^{1}/_{2}$
     Signed lower center: C. Prendergast
     Lent by Mrs. Anne Burnett Windfohr

48   FLORIDA GROVE, circa 1945–46.
     $17^{1}/_{2} \times 20$
     Signed lower left: C. Prendergast
     Lent by Mrs. Charles Prendergast

49   INTERIOR, FLORIDA, 1946.
     $10 \times 11^{1}/_{2}$
     Signed lower left: C. Prendergast
     Lent by Mrs. Charles Prendergast

50   GLORY BOWER, 1946–47.
     $15 \times 21$
     Signed lower left: C. Prendergast
     Anonymous loan

**Screen**

51   SCREEN, 1916–17.
     $75 \times 82^{1}/_{2}$
     Unsigned
     Lent by Mrs. Duncan Phillips
     (Color plates, pp. 15, 16)

48

52

## Chests

52   CARVED AND DECORATED CHEST, circa 1915.
     H. 22$^{1}/_{2}$, L. 63, D. 17$^{1}/_{2}$
     Signed on back. Upper left corner: C. Prendergast.
     Lent by Mrs. Bliss Parkinson
     (Color plates, see front and back cover.) (Boston only.)

53   CARVED AND DECORATED CHEST, 1926–27.
     H. 19$^{5}/_{8}$, L. 51$^{3}/_{4}$, D. 19$^{1}/_{4}$
     Signed lower left front panel: C. Prendergast
     Lent by the Museum of Fine Arts, Boston
     (Color plate, p. 35)

## Paintings on Glass

54    DECORATED MIRROR WITH TWO FIGURES, circa 1915–16.
$18^{1}/_{4} \times 31$
Unsigned
Lent by Mrs. Charles Prendergast

55    DECORATION ON GLASS, circa 1917.
$19^{1}/_{2} \times 25^{1}/_{2}$
Unsigned
Lent by Mrs. Charles Prendergast

56    THE ZOO, circa 1920.
$13^{1}/_{2} \times 21^{1}/_{2}$
Signed lower right: C. P.
Lent by Mr. and Mrs. Philip F. Newman

## Sculpture

57    EVE, circa 1912–14.
H. $11^{1}/_{2}$
Unsigned
Lent by Mrs. Charles Prendergast

58    ANGEL, circa 1915.
H. 7
Unsigned
Lent by Mrs. Charles Prendergast

59    NUDE, circa 1915.
H. $9^{1}/_{4}$
Unsigned
Lent by Ira and Nancy Glackens

58

60  MAN DANCING, circa 1917.
    H. 8
    Unsigned
    Lent by Mrs. Charles Prendergast

61  KNEELING FIGURE, 1940.
    H. 8
    Signed on base: C. Prendergast
    Lent by Dr. and Mrs. Harold Genvert

62  DOLPHIN, circa 1944.
    H. 4, L. 7
    Signed on pedestal: C. Prendergast
    Lent by Mrs. Hamilton Basso

## Boxes

63  BOX, 1932.
    H. $2^3/_4$, L. $7^1/_2$, W. $3^1/_2$
    Unsigned
    Lent by Mrs. Charles Prendergast

64  SMALL CHEST, circa 1934.
    H. 4, L. 10, W. 7
    Signed inside cover, lower right: C. Prendergast
    Lent by Mrs. Charles Prendergast

65  BOX, circa 1934.
    H. $2^3/_4$, L. $5^3/_4$, W. 4
    Signed inside cover, lower right: monogram C. P.
    Lent by Mrs. Charles Prendergast

98

63

64

## Mosaic

66    MOSAIC, circa 1916–18.
Glass tiles; $39 \times 47^1/_2$
Unsigned
Lent by the Museum of Fine Arts, Boston
(Color plate, p. 36)

## Watercolors

67    ST. PAUL DE VENCE, 1927.
Watercolor on paper; $7 \times 11^1/_2$
Unsigned
Lent by Mrs. Charles Prendergast

68    ANTIBES, 1927.
Watercolor on paper; $10 \times 13$
Signed lower left: C. P. per E. P.
Lent by Mrs. Charles Prendergast

69    HILLTOWN (CANNES), 1927.
Watercolor on paper; $8^5/_8 \times 10^3/_4$
Signed lower right: C. P. per E. P.
Reverse: HILLTOWN (ST. PAUL DE VENCE), 1927. (not illus.)
Signed lower left: C. P. per E. P., $8 \times 10^{11}/_{16}$
Lent by Wadsworth Atheneum, Hartford

70    GRASSE, 1927.
Watercolor on paper; $9 \times 12^1/_4$
Signed lower right: C. Prendergast
Lent by Mr. John Brady, Jr.

71    SKETCH FOR POLO PLAYERS No. 1, circa 1941.
Watercolor and pencil on paper; $20 \times 23^1/_4$
Unsigned
Lent by Mrs. Charles Prendergast

**68**

**69**

72 GROCERY STORE, 1947.
   Watercolor on paper; $8^1/_2 \times 10^3/_4$
   Signed lower left: C. P.
   Lent by the Estate of Mrs. R. Barclay Scull


## Frames and Framed Mirrors

73 CARVED FRAME, 1903.
   $44^7/_8 \times 81^3/_4$
   Signed and dated on back: Charles E. Prendergast, Maurice B. Prendergast 1903
   Commissioned by Mr. Thomas W. Lawson.
   Lent by Mr. and Mrs. Frederick L. Good, Jr.

74 CARVED FRAME, 1909.
   $34^3/_8 \times 39^3/_8$
   Signed and dated on back: C. P. 1909
   Lent by the Museum of Fine Arts, Boston

75 MIRROR WITH FOUR ANGELS' HEADS, circa 1912.
   $22 \times 16$
   Unsigned
   Lent by Mrs. Charles Prendergast

76 CARVED FRAME – BLUE, ROSE, AND GOLD, circa 1912.
   $21^1/_2 \times 17^1/_2$
   Unsigned
   Lent by Mr. and Mrs. Granville M. Brumbaugh

77 MIRROR – BLUE AND GOLD, circa 1912.
   $22 \times 17$
   Unsigned
   Lent by Mrs. Charles Prendergast

73

77

**Frames (on works by Maurice Prendergast)**

78 CARVED FRAME
17 x 23$^1/_2$
Lent by Mrs. Charles Prendergast

79 CARVED FRAME
12 x 19$^1/_2$
Lent by Mrs. Charles Prendergast

80 CARVED AND PAINTED FRAME (DECORATION ON GLASS BY MAURICE PRENDERGAST), circa 1914.
21$^1/_2$ x 11$^1/_2$
Lent by Mrs. Charles Prendergast

81 CARVED FRAME
34$^1/_2$ x 31$^1/_2$
Lent by the Museum of Fine Arts, Boston

78

**80**